Night Prayer

From the Liturgy of the Hours

United States Conference of Catholic Bishops
Washington, D.C.

Concordat cum originali:
Rev. Msgr. James P. Moroney
Executive Director, Secretariat for the Liturgy

Published by authority of the U.S. Catholic Bishops'
Committee on the Liturgy, United States Conference
of Catholic Bishops.

First printing of revised edition, December 1996
Third printing, October 2002

ISBN 1-57455-148-5

CONTENTS

Introduction v

Sunday 1

Monday 8

Tuesday 15

Wednesday 21

Thursday 28

Friday 34

Saturday 41

Appendix I: Prayers for Forgiveness 48

Appendix II: Antiphons in Honor
    of the Blessed Virgin 57

Appendix III: Poetry Selections 61

ACKNOWLEDGMENTS

The International Committee on English in the Liturgy, Inc., is grateful to the following for permission to reproduce copyright material:

Hymns

Benedictine Nuns of Saint Mary's Abbey, West Malling, Sussex, for "We praise you, Father, for your gift."

Geoffrey Chapman Publishers, for James Quinn, SJ, "Day is done but love unfailing," "Now at the daylight's ending."

Faber Music Ltd., London, from *New Catholic Hymnal* Copyright © 1971, "This world, my God, is held within your hand" (text by Hamish Swanston).

Jerome Leaman, for "Lord Jesus Christ, abide with us."

Religious Poetry

William Heinemann Ltd., London, for Arthur Symons, "Lines Written in Her Breviary: Let Nothing Disturb Thee," and "If, Lord, Thy Love for Me Is Strong," from the *Poems of Arthur Symons*.

Oxford University Press, London, for "O Deus Ego Amo Te" from *Poems of Gerard Manley Hopkins* (4th edition) edited by W. H. Gardner and N. H. Mackenzie, published by Oxford University Press by arrangement with the Society of Jesus.

Rainer Maria Rilke, "You, neighbor God, if sometimes in the night," from *Poems from the Book of Hours*, translated by Babette Deutsch. Copyright © 1941 by New Directions Publishing Corporation. Reprinted by permission of New Directions Publishing Corporation.

Psalms

Permission has been granted by the Grail (England) for inclusion of psalms from: *The Psalms: A New Translation* Copyright © the Grail (England) 1963.

The complete Psalms first published in 1963 by and available through Wm. Collins Sons & Co., Limited. In North America through the Paulist Press Inc. and Collins and World.

INTRODUCTION

It is the right and duty of every baptized Christian to pray without ceasing (1 Thessalonians 5:17), offering praise and thanksgiving to God through Christ. We turn to God to ask for all we need, trusting that our prayers will be heard (Matthew 7:11). As the people of God, we pray throughout the day, dedicating time and all human activity to God, the source of all life.

Night Prayer is, therefore, a part of the rhythm of daily prayer for many Catholics. Sometimes, this prayer has taken on a very personal character, composed of one's own select prayers. In other cases, it has become the common prayer which a particular group, such as the family, prays at the end of the day.

This book offers individuals and groups the opportunity to pray Night Prayer taken from the Liturgy of the Hours as restored by the Second Vatican Council. The Liturgy of the Hours is "so arranged that the whole course of the day and night is made holy by the praises of God" (*Constitution on the Sacred Liturgy*, no. 84). As an excerpt from the Liturgy of the Hours, Night Prayer offers all of the faithful the possibility of participating in the prayer of the Church, praying in union with Christ to the Father:

> In this prayer of praise we lift up our hearts to the Father of our Lord Jesus Christ, bringing with us the anguish and hopes, the joys and the sorrows of all our brothers and sisters in the world.
>
> . . . Through this prayer of Christ to which we give voice, our day is sanctified, our activities transformed, our actions made holy. We pray the same psalms that Jesus prayed and come into personal contact with him—the person to whom all Scripture points, the goal to which all history is directed. (Pope John Paul II, Saint Patrick's Cathedral, New York, October 3, 1979)

Night Prayer as found in the Liturgy of the Hours is the last prayer of the day, said just before going to bed, no matter the time. It may be prayed with others—a practice highly encouraged—or alone. A father or mother could, for example, lead the family in this Night Prayer before the children go to bed.

The structure of Night Prayer is designed to allow us to give thanks for and reflect on the day just past and to entrust ourselves to the Lord's care throughout the night. Table I gives an outline of the structure of Night Prayer, whether prayed individually or as a group.

INTRODUCTION

Like the other hours of the Liturgy of the Hours, Night Prayer begins with the introductory verse *God, come to my assistance* and the *Glory to the Father,* to which the *Alleluia* is added outside of Lent. The introduction is a call to prayer and a brief expression of confidence in the Lord's saving help.

EXAMINATION OF CONSCIENCE

Immediately after the introduction there is an examination of conscience. Those praying Night Prayer may wish to pause for silent reflection, reviewing the day's activities in light of Gospel teaching. In communal celebrations a penitential rite, as at Mass, may be used (see Appendix I). When prayed alone, the time of reflection might be followed by a short penitential prayer (see Appendix I).

HYMN

An appropriate hymn follows to set the tone of Night Prayer: praise to God who has given us the gift of this day and who keeps us safe through the night. Hymns are provided in place within this book; others may be substituted, but care should be taken that they fit into the context of Night Prayer.

When Night Prayer is prayed in common, the hymn should be sung. In private recitation of Night Prayer, the hymn may be recited or replaced by an appropriate poem (see Appendix III).

PSALMODY

The psalms are the heart of the Liturgy of the Hours and have been carefully chosen to correspond to the hour of the day. In Night Prayer psalms have been selected that evoke confidence in God. Although each day has a selected psalm or psalms, one may always substitute the Saturday or Sunday psalms on weekdays; this might be helpful for those who would like to pray Night Prayer from memory. When celebrating solemnities that do not fall on Sunday (see Table II), the Saturday psalms should be used the day before the solemnity and the Sunday psalms should be used on the day itself.

The psalm concludes with the *Glory to the Father,* giving the prayer of the Old Testament a quality of praise as well as adding a christological and trinitarian dimension.

An antiphon is provided for each psalm and serves to briefly state the theme of the psalm, often highlighting a certain significant phrase that might easily be missed. On occasion (especially when prayed by a group) the antiphon may be used as a response after each verse of the psalm, in the manner of the responsorial psalm of the liturgy of the word in the eucharist.

A title is given at the beginning of each psalm to explain the christological meaning of the psalm. This title is an aid to prayer and is not intended to be read aloud.

READING AND RESPONSORY

A short reading from scripture follows the psalm and should be read and received as a true proclamation of God's word. The passages chosen for Night Prayer are appropriate for the time of day as they refer to images such as night, sleep, and rest.

The response to the reading may be twofold: silent reflection and the responsory *Into your hands*. The response enables God's word to penetrate more deeply into the minds and hearts of those who are praying.

GOSPEL CANTICLE

The Canticle of Simeon (Luke 2:29-32) is said at Night Prayer throughout the week. This canticle, the climax of Night Prayer, expresses Simeon's faith and confidence in God's wonderful work of salvation: Jesus Christ. The canticle concludes with the *Glory to the Father*.

PRAYER

A concluding prayer, which varies each night, follows immediately. It attempts to sum up the entire intention of Night Prayer in the form of a final petition addressed to God the Father. On solemnities not celebrated on Sundays (see Table II), the alternative prayers given for Saturday and Sunday may be used.

CONCLUSION AND ANTIPHON OF THE BLESSED VIRGIN MARY

After the final prayer, the blessing *May the all-powerful Lord* is said, even when Night Prayer is said alone.

Finally, one of the antiphons in honor of the Blessed Virgin is said (see Appendix II).

Table I
FORMAT OF
NIGHT PRAYER

Introduction (*God, come to my assistance*)
Examination of Conscience
    Silent Reflection
    Penitential Prayer or Penitential Rite
Hymn
Psalmody
Reading
Responsory
Gospel Canticle
Prayer
Conclusion
Antiphon of the Blessed Virgin Mary

Table II
LIST OF SOLEMNITIES

The following solemnities frequently fall on days other than Sunday, though Sunday Night Prayer should be used for these days. The celebration of these solemnities begins the evening before the actual date and Saturday's Night Prayer should be used in these cases (i.e., Night Prayer for Saturday would be prayed on December 31 and Night Prayer for Sunday would be prayed on January 1, regardless of the actual day of the week).

On occasion, these celebrations may be replaced by a celebration of higher rank (e.g., the Annunciation may be replaced by Palm Sunday or a day of Holy Week). For such occurrences, consult a liturgical calendar or ordo that gives the proper dates for all liturgical celebrations in a given year.

Solemnity of Mary, Mother of God (January 1)
Solemnity of Joseph, Husband of Mary (March 19)
Solemnity of the Annunciation (March 25)
Solemnity of the Sacred Heart (Friday following the Second Sunday after Pentecost)
Solemnity of the Birth of John the Baptist (June 24)
Solemnity of Peter and Paul, Apostles (June 29)
Solemnity of the Assumption (August 15)
Solemnity of All Saints (November 1)
Solemnity of the Immaculate Conception (December 8)
Solemnity of Christmas (December 25)

SUNDAY

INTRODUCTION

God, come to my assistance.
—Lord, make haste to help me.

Glory to the Father, and to the Son, and to the
Holy Spirit: as it was in the beginning, is now,
and will be for ever. Amen. Alleluia.

*A brief examination of conscience may be made. At its con-
clusion one of the penitential prayers in Appendix I may be
said.*

HYMN

Now thank we all our God
With hearts and hands and voices,
Who wondrous things has done,
In whom the world rejoices;
Who from our mother's arms
Has blest us on our way
With countless gifts of love,
And still is ours today.

O may this gracious God
Through all our life be near us,
With ever joyful hearts,
And blessed peace to cheer us;
Preserve us in his grace,
And guide us in distress,
And free us from all sin,
Till heaven we possess.

All praise and thanks to God
The Father now be given,
The Son and Spirit blest,
Who reigns in highest heaven;
Eternal, Triune God,
Whom earth and heav'n adore;
For thus it was, is now,
And shall be evermore.

Melody: Nun Danket
Music: Johann Crüger, 1598-1662
67.67.66.66 *Text: Martin Rinkart, 1586-1649*
Translator: Catherine Winkworth, 1827-1878

PSALMODY

Ant.   Night holds no terrors for me sleeping
        under God's wings.

Psalm 91
Safe in God's sheltering care

I have given you the power to tread upon serpents and scorpions (Luke 10:19).

He who dwells in the shelter of the Most High
and abides in the shade of the Almighty
says to the Lord: "My refuge,
my stronghold, my God in whom I trust!"

It is he who will free you from the snare
of the fowler who seeks to destroy you;
he will conceal you with his pinions
and under his wings you will find refuge.

You will not fear the terror of the night
nor the arrow that flies by day,
nor the plague that prowls in the darkness
nor the scourge that lays waste at noon.

A thousand may fall at your side,
ten thousand fall at your right,
you, it will never approach;
his faithfulness is buckler and shield.

Your eyes have only to look
to see how the wicked are repaid,
you who have said: "Lord, my refuge!"
and have made the Most High your dwelling.

Upon you no evil shall fall,
no plague approach where you dwell.
For you has he commanded his angels,
to keep you in all your ways.

They shall bear you upon their hands
lest you strike your foot against a stone.
On the lion and the viper you will tread
and trample the young lion and the dragon.

Since he clings to me in love, I will free him;
protect him for he knows my name.
When he calls I shall answer: "I am with you."
I will save him in distress and give him glory.

With length of life I will content him;
I shall let him see my saving power.

Glory to the Father, and to the Son, and to the
Holy Spirit: as it was in the beginning, is now, and
will be for ever.

Ant.   Night holds no terrors for me sleeping
         under God's wings.

READING   *Revelation 22:4-5*

They shall see the Lord face to face and bear his name on their foreheads. The night shall be no more. They will need no light from lamps or the sun, for the Lord God shall give them light, and they shall reign forever.

RESPONSORY

Into your hands, Lord, I commend my spirit.
—Into your hands, Lord, I commend my spirit.

You have redeemed us, Lord God of truth.
—I commend my spirit.

Glory to the Father, and to the Son, and to the Holy Spirit.
—Into your hands, Lord, I commend my spirit.

GOSPEL CANTICLE   *Luke 2:29-32*

Christ is the light of the nations and the glory of Israel.

Ant.   Protect us, Lord, as we stay awake; watch over us as we sleep, that awake, we may keep watch with Christ, and asleep, rest in his peace.

Lord, now you let your servant go in peace;
your word has been fulfilled:
my own eyes have seen the salvation
which you have prepared in the sight of every
people:
a light to reveal you to the nations
and the glory of your people Israel.

Glory to the Father, and to the Son, and to the
Holy Spirit: as it was in the beginning, is now,
and will be for ever.

Ant. Protect us, Lord, as we stay awake; watch
over us as we sleep, that awake, we may
keep watch with Christ, and asleep, rest in
his peace.

PRAYER

Lord,
we have celebrated today
the mystery of the rising of Christ to new life.
May we now rest in your peace,
safe from all that could harm us,
and rise again refreshed and joyful,
to praise you throughout another day.

We ask this through Christ our Lord.

Or: (on solemnities that do not occur on Sunday)

Lord,
we beg you to visit this house
and banish from it
all the deadly power of the enemy.
May your holy angels dwell here
to keep us in peace,
and may your blessing be upon us always.

We ask this through Christ our Lord.

CONCLUSION

May the all-powerful Lord grant us a restful night
and a peaceful death.
—Amen.

Antiphon of the Blessed Virgin Mary (see Appendix II).

MONDAY

INTRODUCTION

God, come to my assistance.
—Lord, make haste to help me.

> Glory to the Father, and to the Son, and to the
> Holy Spirit: as it was in the beginning, is now,
> and will be for ever. Amen. Alleluia.

A brief examination of conscience may be made. At its con-
clusion one of the penitential prayers in Appendix I may be
said.

HYMN

Day is done, but love unfailing
    Dwells ever here;
Shadows fall, but hope, prevailing,
    Calms every fear.
Loving Father, none forsaking,
Take our hearts, of Love's own making,
Watch our sleeping, guard our waking,
    Be always near.

Dark descends, but Light unending
    Shines through our night;
You are with us, ever lending
    New strength to sight;
One in love, your truth confessing,
One in hope of heaven's blessing,
May we see, in love's possessing,
    Love's endless light!

Eyes will close, but you, unsleeping,
    Watch by our side;
Death may come: in Love's safe keeping
    Still we abide.
God of love, all evil quelling,
Sin forgiving, fear dispelling,
Stay with us, our hearts indwelling,
    This eventide.

Melody: Ar Hyd Y Nos Music: Welsh Traditional Melody
84.84.88.84   Text: James Quinn, SJ, 1968

PSALMODY

Ant.   O Lord, our God, unwearied is your love for us.

Psalm 86
Poor man's prayer in trouble

Blessed be God who comforts us in all our trials (2 Corinthians 1:3, 4).

Turn your ear, O Lord, and give answer
for I am poor and needy.
Preserve my life, for I am faithful:
save the servant who trusts in you.

You are my God; have mercy on me, Lord,
for I cry to you all day long.
Give joy to your servant, O Lord,
for to you I lift up my soul.

O Lord, you are good and forgiving,
full of love to all who call.
Give heed, O Lord, to my prayer
and attend to the sound of my voice.

In the day of distress I will call
and surely you will reply.
Among the gods there is none like you, O Lord;
nor work to compare with yours.

All the nations shall come to adore you
and glorify your name, O Lord:
for you are great and do marvellous deeds,
you who alone are God.

Show me, Lord, your way
so that I may walk in your truth.
Guide my heart to fear your name.

I will praise you, Lord my God, with all my
   heart
and glorify your name for ever;
for your love to me has been great:
you have saved me from the depths of the grave.

The proud have risen against me;
ruthless men seek my life:
to you they pay no heed.

But you, God of mercy and compassion,
slow to anger, O Lord,
abounding in love and truth,
turn and take pity on me.

O give your strength to your servant
and save your handmaid's son.
Show me a sign of your favor
that my foes may see to their shame
that you console me and give me your help.

Glory to the Father, and to the Son, and to the Holy Spirit: as it was in the beginning, is now, and will be for ever.

Ant.   O Lord, our God, unwearied is your love for us.

READING   *1 Thessalonians 5:9-10*

God has destined us for acquiring salvation through our Lord Jesus Christ. He died for us, that all of us, whether awake or asleep, together might live with him.

RESPONSORY

Into your hands, Lord, I commend my spirit.
—Into your hands, Lord, I commend my spirit.

You have redeemed us, Lord God of truth.
—I commend my spirit.

Glory to the Father, and to the Son, and to the Holy Spirit.
—Into your hands, Lord, I commend my spirit.

GOSPEL CANTICLE   *Luke 2:29-32*

Christ is the light of the nations and the glory of Israel.

Ant. Protect us, Lord, as we stay awake; watch over us as we sleep, that awake, we may keep watch with Christ, and asleep, rest in his peace.

Lord, now you let your servant go in peace;
your word has been fulfilled:
my own eyes have seen the salvation
which you have prepared in the sight of every people:
a light to reveal you to the nations
and the glory of your people Israel.

Glory to the Father, and to the Son, and to the Holy Spirit: as it was in the beginning, is now, and will be for ever.

Ant. Protect us, Lord, as we stay awake; watch over us as we sleep, that awake, we may keep watch with Christ, and asleep, rest in his peace.

13

PRAYER

Lord,
give our bodies restful sleep
and let the work we have done today
bear fruit in eternal life.

We ask this through Christ our Lord.

CONCLUSION

May the all-powerful Lord grant us a restful night
    and a peaceful death.
—Amen.

Antiphon of the Blessed Virgin Mary (see Appendix II).

TUESDAY

INTRODUCTION

God, come to my assistance.
—Lord, make haste to help me.

Glory to the Father, and to the Son, and to the
Holy Spirit: as it was in the beginning, is now,
and will be for ever. Amen. Alleluia.

*A brief examination of conscience may be made. At its con-
clusion one of the penitential prayers in Appendix I may be
said.*

HYMN

> This world, my God, is held within your hand,
> Though we forget your love and steadfast
>   might
> And in the changing day uncertain stand,
> Disturbed by morning, and afraid of night.
>
> From youthful confidence to careful age,
> Help us each one to be your loving friend,
> Rewarded by the faithful servant's wage,
> God in three persons, reigning without end.

Melody: In Manus Tuas   *Music: Herbert Howells*
10.10.10.10   *Text: Hamish Swanston*

PSALMODY

Ant.   Do not hide your face from me; in you I
        put my trust.

Psalm 143:1-11
Prayer in distress

*Only by faith in Jesus Christ is a man made holy in God's
sight. No observance of the law can achieve this (Galatians
2:16).*

> Lord, listen to my prayer:
> turn your ear to my appeal.
> You are faithful, you are just; give answer.

Do not call your servant to judgment
for no one is just in your sight.

The enemy pursues my soul;
he has crushed my life to the ground;
he has made me dwell in darkness
like the dead, long forgotten.
Therefore my spirit fails;
my heart is numb within me.

I remember the days that are past:
I ponder all your works.
I muse on what your hand has wrought
and to you I stretch out my hands.
Like a parched land my soul thirsts for you.

Lord, make haste and answer;
for my spirit fails within me.
Do not hide your face
lest I become like those in the grave.

In the morning let me know your love
for I put my trust in you.
Make me know the way I should walk:
to you I lift up my soul.

Rescue me, Lord, from my enemies;
I have fled to you for refuge.
Teach me to do your will
for you, O Lord, are my God.
Let your good spirit guide me
in ways that are level and smooth.

For your name's sake, Lord, save my life;
in your justice save my soul from distress.

Glory to the Father, and to the Son, and to the
Holy Spirit: as it was in the beginning, is now,
and will be for ever.

Ant.   Do not hide your face from me; in you I
put my trust.

READING   *1 Peter 5:8-9a*

Stay sober and alert. Your opponent the devil
is prowling like a roaring lion looking for some-
one to devour. Resist him, solid in your faith.

RESPONSORY

Into your hands, Lord, I commend my spirit.
—Into your hands, Lord, I commend my spirit.

You have redeemed us, Lord God of truth.
—I commend my spirit.

Glory to the Father, and to the Son, and to the
Holy Spirit.
—Into your hands, Lord, I commend my spirit.

GOSPEL CANTICLE   *Luke 2:29-32*

Christ is the light of the nations and the glory of Israel.

Ant.   Protect us, Lord, as we stay awake; watch
          over us as we sleep, that awake, we may
          keep watch with Christ, and asleep, rest in
          his peace.

Lord, now you let your servant go in peace;
your word has been fulfilled:
my own eyes have seen the salvation
which you have prepared in the sight of every
          people:
a light to reveal you to the nations
and the glory of your people Israel.

Glory to the Father, and to the Son, and to the
Holy Spirit: as it was in the beginning, is now,
and will be for ever.

Ant.   Protect us, Lord, as we stay awake; watch
          over us as we sleep, that awake, we may
          keep watch with Christ, and asleep, rest in
          his peace.

19

PRAYER

Lord,
fill this night with your radiance.
May we sleep in peace and rise with joy
to welcome the light of a new day in your name.

We ask this through Christ our Lord.

CONCLUSION

May the all-powerful Lord grant us a restful night
and a peaceful death.
—Amen.

Antiphon of the Blessed Virgin Mary (see Appendix II).

WEDNESDAY

INTRODUCTION

God, come to my assistance.
—Lord, make haste to help me.

> Glory to the Father, and to the Son, and to the
> Holy Spirit: as it was in the beginning, is now,
> and will be for ever. Amen. Alleluia.

*A brief examination of conscience may be made. At its con-
clusion one of the penitential prayers in Appendix I may be
said.*

HYMN

Glory to thee, my God, this night,
For all the blessings of the light;
Keep us, O keep me, King of kings,
Beneath thine own almighty wings.

Forgive me, Lord, for thy dear Son,
The sin that I this day have done;
That with the world, myself and thee,
I, before sleep, at peace may be.

O may my soul on thee repose,
And with deep sleep my eyelids close,
The gift of rest I gladly take
To serve my God when I awake.

Melody: Tallis' Canon
Text: Thomas Ken, 1709, alt. L.M.

PSALMODY

Ant. 1 Lord God, be my refuge and my strength.

Psalm 31:1-6
Trustful prayer in adversity

Father, into your hands I commend my spirit (Luke 23:46).

In you, O Lord, I take refuge.
Let me never be put to shame.
In your justice, set me free,
hear me and speedily rescue me.

Be a rock of refuge for me,
a mighty stronghold to save me,
for you are my rock, my stronghold.
For your name's sake, lead me and guide me.

Release me from the snares they have hidden
for you are my refuge, Lord.
Into your hands I commend my spirit.
It is you who will redeem me, Lord.

Glory to the Father, and to the Son, and to the
Holy Spirit: as it was in the beginning, is now,
and will be for ever.

Ant.   Lord God, be my refuge and my strength.

Ant. 2 Out of the depths I cry to you, Lord.

Psalm 130
A cry from the depths

He will save his people from their sins (Matthew 1:21).

Out of the depths I cry to you, O Lord,
Lord, hear my voice!
O let your ears be attentive
to the voice of my pleading.

If you, O Lord, should mark our guilt,
Lord, who would survive?
But with you is found forgiveness:
for this we revere you.

My soul is waiting for the Lord,
I count on his word.
My soul is longing for the Lord
more than watchman for daybreak.
Let the watchman count on daybreak
and Israel on the Lord.

Because with the Lord there is mercy
and fullness of redemption,
Israel indeed he will redeem
from all its iniquity.

Glory to the Father, and to the Son, and to the
Holy Spirit: as it was in the beginning, is now,
and will be for ever.

Ant.   Out of the depths I cry to you, Lord.

READING   *Ephesians 4:26-27*

If you are angry, let it be without sin. The sun must not go down on your wrath; do not give the devil a chance to work on you.

RESPONSORY

Into your hands, Lord, I commend my spirit.
—Into your hands, Lord, I commend my spirit.

You have redeemed us, Lord God of truth.
—I commend my spirit.

Glory to the Father, and to the Son, and to the Holy Spirit.
—Into your hands, Lord, I commend my spirit.

GOSPEL CANTICLE   *Luke 2:29-32*

Christ is the light of the nations and the glory of Israel.

Ant.   Protect us, Lord, as we stay awake; watch over us as we sleep, that awake, we may keep watch with Christ, and asleep, rest in his peace.

Lord, now you let your servant go in peace;
your word has been fulfilled:
my own eyes have seen the salvation
which you have prepared in the sight of every
  people:
a light to reveal you to the nations
and the glory of your people Israel.

Glory to the Father, and to the Son, and to the
Holy Spirit: as it was in the beginning, is now,
and will be for ever.

Ant. Protect us, Lord, as we stay awake; watch
      over us as we sleep, that awake, we may
      keep watch with Christ, and asleep, rest in
      his peace.

PRAYER

Lord Jesus Christ,
you have given your followers
an example of gentleness and humility,
a task that is easy, a burden that is light.
Accept the prayers and work of this day,
and give us the rest that will strengthen us
to render more faithful service to you
who live and reign for ever and ever.

CONCLUSION

May the all-powerful Lord grant us a restful night
and a peaceful death.
—Amen.

Antiphon of the Blessed Virgin Mary (see Appendix II).

THURSDAY

INTRODUCTION

God, come to my assistance.
—Lord, make haste to help me.

Glory to the Father, and to the Son, and to the
Holy Spirit: as it was in the beginning, is now,
and will be for ever. Amen. Alleluia.

*A brief examination of conscience may be made. At its con-
clusion one of the penitential prayers in Appendix I may be
said.*

HYMN

Holy God, we praise thy name!
Lord of all, we bow before thee!
All on earth thy sceptre claim,
All in heav'n above adore thee!
Infinite thy vast domain,
Everlasting is thy reign.

Hark! the loud celestial hymn
Angel choirs above are raising;
Cherubim and seraphim,
In unceasing chorus praising,
Fill the heav'ns with sweet accord:
Holy, holy, holy Lord!

Holy Father, Holy Son,
Holy Spirit, Three we name thee,
While in essence only One,
Undivided God we claim thee;
And adoring bend the knee,
While we own the mystery.

Melody: Grosser Gott
Music: Katholisches Gesangbuch, Vienna, c. 1774
78.78.77   *Text: Ignaz Franz, 1719-1790*
Translator: Clarence Walworth, 1820-1900

PSALMODY

Ant.   In you, my God, my body will rest in hope.

Psalm 16
God is my portion, my inheritance

The Father raised up Jesus from the dead and broke the bonds of death (Acts 2:24).

Preserve me, God, I take refuge in you.
I say to the Lord: "You are my God.
My happiness lies in you alone."

He has put into my heart a marvellous love
for the faithful ones who dwell in his land.
Those who choose other gods increase their
     sorrows.
Never will I offer their offerings of blood.
Never will I take their name upon my lips.

O Lord, it is you who are my portion and cup;
it is you yourself who are my prize.
The lot marked out for me is my delight:
welcome indeed the heritage that falls to me!

I will bless the Lord who gives me counsel,
who even at night directs my heart.
I keep the Lord ever in my sight:
since he is at my right hand, I shall stand firm.

And so my heart rejoices, my soul is glad;
even my body shall rest in safety.
For you will not leave my soul among the dead,
nor let your beloved know decay.

You will show me the path of life,
the fullness of joy in your presence,
at your right hand happiness for ever.

Glory to the Father, and to the Son, and to the
Holy Spirit: as it was in the beginning, is now,
and will be for ever.

Ant.   In you, my God, my body will rest in hope.

READING   *1 Thessalonians 5:23*

May the God of peace make you perfect in
holiness. May he preserve you whole and entire,
spirit, soul, and body, irreproachable at the coming of our Lord Jesus Christ.

RESPONSORY

Into your hands, Lord, I commend my spirit.
—Into your hands, Lord, I commend my spirit.

You have redeemed us, Lord God of truth.
—I commend my spirit.

Glory to the Father, and to the Son, and to the
   Holy Spirit.
—Into your hands, Lord, I commend my spirit.

GOSPEL CANTICLE   *Luke 2:29-32*

Christ is the light of the nations and the glory of Israel.

Ant.   Protect us, Lord, as we stay awake; watch
       over us as we sleep, that awake, we may
       keep watch with Christ, and asleep, rest in
       his peace.

Lord, now you let your servant go in peace;
your word has been fulfilled:
my own eyes have seen the salvation
which you have prepared in the sight of every
   people:
a light to reveal you to the nations
and the glory of your people Israel.

Glory to the Father, and to the Son, and to the
Holy Spirit: as it was in the beginning, is now,
and will be for ever.

Ant.   Protect us, Lord, as we stay awake; watch
       over us as we sleep, that awake, we may
       keep watch with Christ, and asleep, rest in
       his peace.

PRAYER

Lord God,
send peaceful sleep
to refresh our tired bodies.
May your help always renew us
and keep us strong in your service.

We ask this through Christ our Lord.

CONCLUSION

May the all-powerful Lord grant us a restful night
    and a peaceful death.
—Amen.

Antiphon of the Blessed Virgin Mary (see Appendix II).

FRIDAY

INTRODUCTION

God, come to my assistance.
—Lord, make haste to help me.

> Glory to the Father, and to the Son, and to the
> Holy Spirit: as it was in the beginning, is now,
> and will be for ever. Amen. Alleluia.

A brief examination of conscience may be made. At its con-
clusion one of the penitential prayers in Appendix I may be
said.

HYMN

Lord Jesus Christ, abide with us,
Now that the sun has run its course;
Let hope not be obscured by night,
But may faith's darkness be as light.

Lord Jesus Christ, grant us your peace,
And when the trials of earth shall cease,
Grant us the morning light of grace,
The radiant splendor of your face.

Immortal, Holy, Threefold Light,
Yours be the kingdom, pow'r, and might;
All glory be eternally
To you, life-giving Trinity!

Melody: Old 100th L.M.
Music: Louis Bourgeois, 1551
Text: Saint Joseph's Abbey, 1967, 1968

PSALMODY

Ant.   Day and night I cry to you, my God.

Psalm 88
Prayer of a sick person

This is your hour when darkness reigns (Luke 22:53).

Lord my God, I call for help by day;
I cry at night before you.
Let my prayer come into your presence.
O turn your ear to my cry.

For my soul is filled with evils;
my life is on the brink of the grave.
I am reckoned as one in the tomb:
I have reached the end of my strength,

like one alone among the dead;
like the slain lying in their graves;
like those you remember no more,
cut off, as they are, from your hand.

You have laid me in the depths of the tomb,
in places that are dark, in the depths.
Your anger weighs down upon me:
I am drowned beneath your waves.

You have taken away my friends
and made me hateful in their sight.
Imprisoned, I cannot escape;
my eyes are sunken with grief.

I call to you, Lord, all the day long;
to you I stretch out my hands.
Will you work your wonders for the dead?
Will the shades stand and praise you?

Will your love be told in the grave
or your faithfulness among the dead?
Will your wonders be known in the dark
or your justice in the land of oblivion?

As for me, Lord, I call to you for help:
in the morning my prayer comes before you.
Lord, why do you reject me?
Why do you hide your face?

Wretched, close to death from my youth,
I have borne your trials; I am numb.
Your fury has swept down upon me;
your terrors have utterly destroyed me.

They surround me all the day like a flood,
they assail me all together.
Friend and neighbor you have taken away:
my one companion is darkness.

Glory to the Father, and to the Son, and to the Holy Spirit: as it was in the beginning, is now, and will be for ever.

Ant.   Day and night I cry to you, my God.

READING   *Jeremiah 14:9a*

You are in our midst, O Lord,
    your name we bear:
    do not forsake us, O Lord, our God!

RESPONSORY

Into your hands, Lord, I commend my spirit.
—Into your hands, Lord, I commend my spirit.

You have redeemed us, Lord God of truth.
—I commend my spirit.

Glory to the Father, and to the Son, and to the Holy Spirit.
—Into your hands, Lord, I commend my spirit.

GOSPEL CANTICLE   *Luke 2:29-32*

Christ is the light of the nations and the glory of Israel.

Ant.   Protect us, Lord, as we stay awake; watch
over us as we sleep, that awake, we may
keep watch with Christ, and asleep, rest in
his peace.

Lord, now you let your servant go in peace;
your word has been fulfilled:
my own eyes have seen the salvation
which you have prepared in the sight of every
    people:
a light to reveal you to the nations
and the glory of your people Israel.

Glory to the Father, and to the Son, and to the
Holy Spirit: as it was in the beginning, is now,
and will be for ever.

Ant.   Protect us, Lord, as we stay awake; watch
over us as we sleep, that awake, we may
keep watch with Christ, and asleep, rest in
his peace.

PRAYER

All-powerful God,
keep us united with your Son
in his death and burial
so that we may rise to new life with him,
who lives and reigns for ever and ever.

CONCLUSION

May the all-powerful Lord grant us a restful night
and a peaceful death.
—Amen.

Antiphon of the Blessed Virgin Mary (see Appendix II).

SATURDAY

INTRODUCTION

God, come to my assistance.
—Lord, make haste to help me.

> Glory to the Father, and to the Son, and to the
> Holy Spirit: as it was in the beginning, is now,
> and will be for ever. Amen. Alleluia.

*A brief examination of conscience may be made. At its con-
clusion one of the penitential prayers in Appendix I may be
said.*

HYMN

We praise you, Father, for your gifts
Of dusk and nightfall over earth,
Foreshadowing the mystery
Of death that leads to endless day.

Within your hands we rest secure;
In quiet sleep our strength renew;
Yet give your people hearts that wake
In love to you, unsleeping Lord.

Your glory may we ever seek
In rest, as in activity,
Until its fullness is revealed,
O source of life, O Trinity.

Melody: Te lucis ante terminum (plainchant)
Music: Anon., Gregorian
Text: West Malling Abbey

PSALMODY

Ant. 1 Have mercy, Lord, and hear my prayer.

Psalm 4
Thanksgiving

The resurrection of Christ was God's supreme and wholly marvelous work (Saint Augustine).

When I call, answer me, O God of justice;
from anguish you released me; have mercy and
hear me!

O men, how long will your hearts be closed,
will you love what is futile and seek what is
false?

It is the Lord who grants favors to those whom
he loves;
the Lord hears me whenever I call him.

Fear him; do not sin; ponder on your bed and
be still.
Make justice your sacrifice and trust in the
Lord.

"What can bring us happiness?" many say.
Let the light of your face shine on us, O Lord.

You have put into my heart a greater joy
than they have from abundance of corn and
new wine.

I will lie down in peace and sleep comes at once
for you alone, Lord, make me dwell in safety.

Glory to the Father, and to the Son, and to the
Holy Spirit: as it was in the beginning, is now,
and will be for ever.

Ant.   Have mercy, Lord, and hear my prayer.

Ant. 2 In the silent hours of night, bless the Lord.

Psalm 134
Evening prayer in the Temple

*Praise our God, all you his servants, you who fear him, small
and great (Revelation 19:5).*

O come, bless the Lord,
all you who serve the Lord,
who stand in the house of the Lord,
in the courts of the house of our God.

Lift up your hands to the holy place
and bless the Lord through the night.

May the Lord bless you from Zion,
he who made both heaven and earth.

Glory to the Father, and to the Son, and to the
Holy Spirit: as it was in the beginning, is now,
and will be for ever.

Ant. In the silent hours of night, bless the Lord.

READING   *Deuteronomy 6:4-7*

Hear, O Israel! The Lord is our God, the Lord
alone! Therefore, you shall love the Lord, your
God, with all your heart, and with all your soul,
and with all your strength. Take to heart these
words which I enjoin on you today. Drill them into
your children. Speak of them at home and abroad,
whether you are busy or at rest.

RESPONSORY

Into your hands, Lord, I commend my spirit.
—Into your hands, Lord, I commend my spirit.

You have redeemed us, Lord God of truth.
—I commend my spirit.

Glory to the Father, and to the Son, and to the
   Holy Spirit.
—Into your hands, Lord, I commend my spirit.

GOSPEL CANTICLE   *Luke 2:29-32*

Christ is the light of the nations and the glory of Israel.

Ant.   Protect us, Lord, as we stay awake; watch over us as we sleep, that awake, we may keep watch with Christ, and asleep, rest in his peace.

Lord, now you let your servant go in peace;
your word has been fulfilled:
my own eyes have seen the salvation
which you have prepared in the sight of every
     people:
a light to reveal you to the nations
and the glory of your people Israel.

Glory to the Father, and to the Son, and to the Holy Spirit: as it was in the beginning, is now, and will be for ever.

Ant.   Protect us, Lord, as we stay awake; watch over us as we sleep, that awake, we may keep watch with Christ, and asleep, rest in his peace.

46

PRAYER

Lord,
be with us throughout this night.
When day comes may we rise from sleep
to rejoice in the resurrection of your Christ,
who lives and reigns for ever and ever.

Or: (on the night before solemnities that do not occur on Sunday)

Lord,
we beg you to visit this house
and banish from it
all the deadly power of the enemy.
May your holy angels dwell here
to keep us in peace,
and may your blessing be upon us always.

We ask this through Christ our Lord.

CONCLUSION

May the all-powerful Lord grant us a restful night
    and a peaceful death.
—Amen.

Antiphon of the Blessed Virgin Mary (see Appendix II).

Appendix I
PRAYERS FOR FORGIVENESS

WHEN NIGHT PRAYER IS PRAYED ALONE

A brief pause for reflection might be followed by one of the following short penitential prayers:

1.

My God,
I am sorry for my sins with all my heart.
In choosing to do wrong
and failing to do good,
I have sinned against you
whom I should love above all things.
I firmly intend, with your help,
to do penance,
to sin no more,
and to avoid whatever leads me to sin.
Our Savior Jesus Christ
suffered and died for us.
In his name, my God, have mercy.

2.

Remember, Lord, your compassion and mercy
which you showed long ago.
Do not recall the sins and failings of my youth.
In your mercy remember me, Lord, because of your
    goodness.

Psalm 25:6-7

3.

Wash me from my guilt
and cleanse me of my sin.
I acknowledge my offense;
my sin is before me always.

Psalm 51:4-5

4.

Lord Jesus,
you chose to be called the friend of sinners.
By your saving death and resurrection
free me from my sins.
May your peace take root in my heart
and bring forth a harvest
of love, holiness, and truth.

5.

Father of mercy,
like the prodigal son
I return to you and say:
"I have sinned against you
and am no longer worthy to be called your son."
Christ Jesus, Savior of the World,
I pray with the repentant thief
to whom you promised Paradise:
"Lord, remember me in your kingdom."
Holy Spirit, fountain of love,
I call on you with trust:
"Purify my heart,
and help me to walk as a child of light."

6.

Lord Jesus Christ,
you are the Lamb of God;
you take away the sins of the world.
Through the grace of the Holy Spirit
restore me to friendship with your Father,
cleanse me from every stain of sin
in the blood you shed for me,
and raise me to new life
for the glory of your name.

WHEN NIGHT PRAYER
IS PRAYED IN A GROUP

The leader invites all to recall their sins and to repent of them in silence. He/she may use these or similar words:

Coming together as God's family,
with confidence let us ask the Father's forgiveness,
for he is full of gentleness and compassion.

A.

All say:
I confess to almighty God,
and to you, my brothers and sisters,
that I have sinned through my own fault

> They strike their breast.

in my thoughts and in my words,
in what I have done,
and in what I have failed to do;
and I ask blessed Mary, ever virgin,
all the angels and saints,
and you, my brothers and sisters,
to pray for me to the Lord our God.

The leader then says:
May almighty God have mercy on us,
forgive us our sins,
and bring us to everlasting life.

51

All answer:
Amen.

B.

The leader says:
Lord, we have sinned against you:

All answer:
Lord, have mercy.

Leader:
Lord, show us your mercy and love.

All:
And grant us your salvation.

The leader says:
May almighty God have mercy on us,
forgive us our sins,
and bring us to everlasting life.

All answer:
Amen.

C.

The leader makes the following or other invocations:

i.

Leader:
You were sent to heal the contrite:
Lord, have mercy.

All answer:
Lord, have mercy.

Leader:
You came to call sinners:
Christ, have mercy.

All:
Christ, have mercy.

Leader:
You plead for us at the right hand of the Father:
Lord, have mercy.

All:
Lord, have mercy.

The leader says:
May almighty God have mercy on us,
forgive us our sins,
and bring us to everlasting life.

All answer:
Amen.

ii.

Leader:

Lord Jesus, you came to reconcile us
to one another and to the Father:
Lord, have mercy.

All answer:

Lord, have mercy.

Leader:

Lord Jesus, you heal the wounds of sin and division:
Christ, have mercy.

All:

Christ, have mercy.

Leader:

Lord Jesus, you intercede for us with your Father:
Lord, have mercy.

All:

Lord, have mercy.

The leader says:

May almighty God have mercy on us,
forgive us our sins,
and bring us to everlasting life.

All answer:

Amen.

iii.

Leader:
You raise the dead to life in the Spirit:
Lord, have mercy.

All answer:
Lord, have mercy.

Leader:
You bring pardon and peace to the sinner:
Christ, have mercy.

All:
Christ, have mercy.

Leader:
You bring light to those in darkness:
Lord, have mercy.

All:
Lord, have mercy.

The leader says:
May almighty God have mercy on us,
forgive us our sins,
and bring us to everlasting life.

All answer:
Amen.

iv.

Leader:
Lord Jesus, you healed the sick:
Lord, have mercy.

All answer:
Lord, have mercy.

Leader:
Lord Jesus, you forgave sinners:
Christ, have mercy.

All:
Christ, have mercy.

Leader:
Lord Jesus, you give us yourself to heal us and bring
    us strength:
Lord, have mercy.

All:
Lord, have mercy.

The leader says:
May almighty God have mercy on us,
forgive us our sins,
and bring us to everlasting life.

All answer:
Amen.

Appendix II
ANTIPHONS IN HONOR OF THE BLESSED VIRGIN

1.

Hail, holy Queen, mother of mercy,
our life, our sweetness, and our hope.
To you do we cry,
poor banished children of Eve.
To you do we send up our sighs
mourning and weeping in this vale of tears.
Turn then, most gracious advocate,
your eyes of mercy toward us,
and after this exile
show us the blessed fruit of your womb, Jesus.
O clement, O loving,
O sweet Virgin Mary.

Salve, Regina, mater misericordiæ;
  vita, dulcedo et spes nostra, salve.
Ad te clamamus, exsules filii Evæ.
Ad te suspiramus, gementes et flentes
  in hac lacrimarum valle.

Eia ergo, advocata nostra,
  illos tuos misericordes oculos
  ad nos converte.
Et Iesum, benedictum fructum ventris tui,
  nobis post hoc exilium ostende.
O clemens, o pia, o dulcis Virgo Maria.

2.

Loving mother of the Redeemer,
gate of heaven, star of the sea,
assist your people who have fallen yet strive to rise
  again.

To the wonderment of nature you bore your
  Creator,
yet remained a virgin after as before.
You who received Gabriel's joyful greeting,
have pity on us poor sinners.

Alma Redemptoris Mater, quæ pervia cæli
    porta manes, et stella maris, succurre cadenti,
surgere qui curat, populo: tu quæ genuisti,
    natura mirante, tuum sanctum Genitorem,
Virgo prius ac posterius, Gabrielis ab ore
    sumens illud Ave, peccatorum miserere.

3.

Hail Mary, full of grace,
the Lord is with you!
Blessed are you among women,
and blessed is the fruit of your womb, Jesus.
Holy Mary, Mother of God,
pray for us sinners,
now and at the hour of our death.

Ave Maria,
gratia plena, Dominus tecum,
benedicta tu in mulieribus,
et benedictus fructus ventris tui, Iesus.
Sancta Maria, Mater Dei,
ora pro nobis peccatoribus,
nunc et in hora mortis nostræ.
Amen.

4.

(To be used between Easter and Pentecost only)

Queen of heaven, rejoice, alleluia.
The Son whom you merited to bear, alleluia,
has risen as he said, alleluia.

Rejoice and be glad, O Virgin Mary, alleluia!
For the Lord has truly risen, alleluia.

Regina cæli, lætare, alleluia,
    quia quem meruisti portare, alleluia,
resurrexit sicut dixit, alleluia;
    ora pro nobis Deum, alleluia.

Gaude et lætare, Virgo Maria, alleluia.
Quia surrexit Dominus vere, alleluia.

Appendix III
POETRY
SELECTIONS

ABIDE WITH ME

Abide with me; fast falls the eventide;
The darkness deepens; Lord, with me abide;
When other helpers fail, and comforts flee,
Help of the helpless, O abide with me.

Swift to its close ebbs out life's little day;
Earth's joys grow dim, its glories pass away;
Change and decay in all around I see;
O thou who changest not, abide with me.

Hold thou thy Cross before my closing eyes;
Shine through the gloom, and point me to the skies;
Heaven's morning breaks, and earth's vain
    shadows flee;
In life, in death, O Lord, abide with me.

H. F. Lyte

LINES WRITTEN IN HER BREVIARY

Let nothing disturb thee,
Nothing affright thee;
All things are passing;
God never changeth;
Patient endurance
Attaineth to all things;
Who God possesseth
In nothing is wanting;
Alone God sufficeth.

Saint Teresa
Translator: Arthur Symons

O DEUS EGO AMO TE

O God, I love thee, I love thee—
Not out of hope of heaven for me
Nor fearing not to love and be
    In the everlasting burning.
Thou, thou, my Jesus, after me
    Didst reach thine arms out dying,
For my sake sufferedst nails and lance,
Mocked and marred countenance,
    Sorrows passing number,
    Sweat and care and cumber,
Yea and death, and this for me,
    And thou couldst see me sinning:
Then I, why should not I love thee,
Jesu, so much in love with me?
Not for heaven's sake; not to be
Out of hell by loving thee;
Not for any gains I see;
But just the way that thou didst me
I do love and I will love thee;
What must I love thee, Lord, for then?
For being my king and God. Amen.

Gerard Manley Hopkins

IF, LORD, THY LOVE FOR ME IS STRONG

If, Lord, Thy love for me is strong
As this which binds me unto Thee,
What holds me from Thee, Lord, so long,
What holds Thee, Lord, so long from me?

O soul, what then desirest thou?
—Lord, I would see, who thus choose Thee.
What fears can yet assail thee now?
—All that I fear is to lose Thee.

Love's whole possession I entreat,
Lord, make my soul Thine own abode,
And I will build a nest so sweet
It may not be too poor for God.

O soul in God hidden from sin,
What more desires for thee remain,
Save but to love, and love again,
And all on flame with love within,
Love on, and turn to love again?

Saint Teresa
Translator: Arthur Symons

LEAD, KINDLY LIGHT

Lead, kindly Light, amid the encircling gloom,
Lead thou me on;
The night is dark, and I am far from home,
Lead thou me on.
Keep thou my feet; I do not ask to see
The distant scene; one step enough for me.

I was not ever thus, nor prayed that thou
Shouldst lead me on;
I loved to choose and see my path; but now
Lead thou me on.
I loved the garish day, and, spite of fears,
Pride ruled my will: remember not past years.

So long thy power hath blest me, sure it still
Will lead me on
O'er moor and fen, o'er crag and torrent, till
The night is gone,
And with the morn those Angel faces smile,
Which I have loved long since, and lost awhile.

J. H. Newman

YOU, NEIGHBOUR GOD

You, neighbour God, if sometimes in the night
I rouse you with loud knocking, I do so
only because I seldom hear you breathe;
And I know: you are alone.
And should you need a drink, no one is there
to reach it to you, groping in the dark.
Always I hearken. Give but a small sign.
I am quite near.

Between us there is but a narrow wall,
and by sheer chance; for it would take
merely a call from your lips or from mine
to break it down,
and that without a sound.

The wall is builded of your images.

They stand before you hiding you like names.
And when the light within me blazes high
that in my inmost soul I know you by,
the radiance is squandered on their frames.

And then my senses, which too soon grow lame,
exiled from you, must go their homeless ways.

Rainer Maria Rilke

PEACE

My soul, there is a country
    Far beyond the stars,
Where stands a wingéd sentry
    All skilful in the wars:
There above noise and danger
    Sweet Peace sits crowned with smiles,
And one born in a manger
    Commands the beauteous files.
He is thy gracious friend
    And—O my soul, awake!—
Did in pure love descend
    To die here for thy sake.
If thou canst get but thither,
    There grows the flower of Peace,
The Rose that cannot wither,
    Thy fortress, and thy ease.
Leave then thy foolish ranges,
    For none can thee secure,
But one who never changes,
    Thy God, thy life, thy cure.

Henry Vaughan

THERE

There, in that other world, what waits for me?
What shall I find after that other birth?
No stormy, tossing, foaming, smiling sea,
    But a new earth.

No sun to mark the changing of the days,
No slow, soft falling of the alternate night,
No moon, no star, no light upon my ways,
    Only the Light.

No gray cathedral, wide and wondrous fair,
That I may tread where all my fathers trod,
Nay, nay, my soul, no house of God is there,
    But only God.

Mary Coleridge